From Orphan to Overcomer

The amazing story of triumph over tragedy

by Ruth Mwagalwa

From Orphan to Overcomer
Copyright © 2014 Ruth Mwagalwa

All rights reserved. No part of this publication may be reproduced, stored in a retrieval system, or transmitted in any form or by any means—electronic, mechanical, photocopying, recording, or otherwise—without the prior written permission of the publisher and copyright owners.

Printed in the United States of America.

eBook: 978-1-312-13016-6
Softcover: 978-1-365-80925-5
Hardcover: 978-1-365-77480-5

Table of Contents

DEDICATION 5

ACKNOWLEDGEMENTS 7

FOREWORD 9

CHAPTER 1 – BIRTH AND CHILDHOOD 11

CHAPTER 2 – ORPHANED AT NINE 15

CHAPTER 3 – PREGNANT AT FIFTEEN 24

CHAPTER 4 – PROSTITUTION 34

CHAPTER 5 – SERIOUS RELATIONSHIP 38

CHAPTER 6 – SAVED! 45

CHAPTER 7 – WIDOWED 49

CHAPTER 8 – AIDS 53

CHAPTER 9 – HEALED 57

CHAPTER 10 – A MINISTRY IS BORN 63

CHAPTER 11 – OFF TO ENGLAND 69

CHAPTER 12 – TODAY AND TOMORROW 73

Dedication

I lovingly dedicate this book to God the Father, the Son and the Holy Spirit, who knew me before I was in my mother's womb, saved me and put me in His vineyard. Lord, you have been by my side even in the darkness. Thank you.

Acknowledgements

I acknowledge with great appreciation several people who have made a significant impact on my life.

Thank you Eddie and Dr. Alice Smith with the U.S. Prayer Center in Houston, Texas (USA) for encouraging me not to die with this book in my heart. You provided me with all of the support I needed to write and publish my story. Thank you so much.

Thank you Asha, Datva, and Deborah (my dear children) who endured the hardships of being raised by a single mother, you are my heroes. I love you.

Thank you to all of God's servants, men and women, who accepted me as a coworker in the Father's vineyard.

Thank you Mrs Olivia Musisi for taking my hand when I was at a cross roads. You showed me the way to fight for my rights.

Thank you Pastor Frida Serwadda for standing with me to start our Widows Intercessors Ministry.

Thank you Mr. John and Rev. Christine Reading and family. You have been a great pillar for our ministry.

Thank you Pastor June Richards, and Mrs. Jane Sullivan for your great support.

I don't have space to mention all of those who have prayed for and supported me. Thank you, and God bless you!

Foreword

I met Pastor Ruth through a Christian ministry friend, Mrs. Chris Reading from the U.K. In 2009 Chris invited me to bring a team to partner with her in ministry in the nation of Uganda. I felt quite drawn to go minister to people in a nation about which I knew little.

The moment I met Ruth I realized that she was authentic--the real deal. Her compassion and dedication to the widows and orphans of her nation is extraordinary. Perhaps one reason is that Ruth has been both an orphan and a widow. She understands the hardships and pain they experience.

Ruth is not only deeply loved and highly respected by the widows of Uganda, but is also honored by pastors, leaders and politicians. I was so impressed with Ruth and her organization that I've returned with ministry teams three times. I sincerely recommend this book to you. Her's is a remarkable story of commitment, courage and conquest.

Dr. Alice Smith
U.S. Prayer Center
Houston, Texas USA

CHAPTER 1 – Birth and Childhood

I was born in Saza, Mityana District, Uganda, which is an African nation. My parents had eight children, four boys and four girls. They were from the nation of Rwanda. They had come, like many other Rwandans, to Uganda looking for jobs. However, when they arrived they were treated badly.

They eventually landed in the hands of a Muslim family, and my father was offered a job in their sugar cane farm. The family loved my father because he was hard-working, and they gave him a piece of land with a chance to work as he pays for it. My parents both worked almost as slaves yet they earned little more than food. The Muslim family tried to convert my father to Islam, but he refused because he considered himself a Roman Catholic.

Not long after I was born my father applied for a job as a cleaner in Mityana Hospital. My mother worked at home tending the family garden with us children. We grew our own food, which included cassava (a root crop similar to a potato), maize (corn), sweet potatoes, beans, coffee and bananas. These are popular foods in Uganda.

What I remember most about my childhood was the level of our poverty. All eight of us children, boys and girls, slept on the same mattress on the floor. Our mattress was a bag we filled with grass clippings. We had no sheets or pillows. We had only pieces of sackcloth, which in the U.S. is known as burlap. It's a rough, material woven (in Uganda) out of a tree. I was fearful of sackcloth because I had only seen people buried in it, so the sight of it reminded me of death. At night I would shiver, shake in fear, and experience nightmares.

The family's two goats also slept in the room with us. This may sound gross, but it illustrates the level of our poverty. The smaller children often wet on "the mattress." At times the smell was unbearable. Our mother would insist that we drag the bedding outside so it could dry in the sun before the next evening. But when dried in the sun, the grass inside the mattress would become matted and hard. It was quite uncomfortable.

I attended Primary-1 School as a child. It wasn't like schools in Western countries. We had no student desks. We sat on the dirt floor. But I loved school, which was at the Full Gospel Church our mother attended. But it was quite a long walking distance from our home. I also enjoyed the church services there because of the clapping, dancing, singing and shouting. It was a lively place.

Sadly our father was a drunkard. He would often sit in front of the house and drink himself into a stupor, then call out to and carry on conversations with his deceased family members. Mother explained to us that what he was doing was bad, but he was doing it because he didn't know God.

Imagine our joy when our father told us one day that he was going to go to church with us. He did, and when we returned home, he took his alcoholic drinks to the church and disposed of them.

Every day we kids would awaken early in the morning, and dig in the garden until it was time to walk to school. When we returned from school, we'd continue digging in the garden until nightfall. It was hard work for children, and we often missed lunch as well as dinner.

This was especially true when mother was pregnant with her eighth baby. She became weak and sick, so sick that father took her to the hospital where he stayed with her. This meant that we seven children were home alone. It was extremely frightening for us. We were fearful that someone would break into our house and hurt us.

I had a deep voice for a young girl. The other children persuaded me that if we heard anyone outside the house at night, I was to disguise my voice and sound manly to scare them off.

The day came when mother gave birth to a baby girl and our father took us to the hospital to visit them. However once there, we discovered that our dear mother was clearly dying. She was on oxygen, and couldn't speak. She just wept. As we each approached her bed, she reached out and touched us. Three days later, she died leaving behind a baby girl of 14 days.

Our father told us that as she was dying she told him, "I'm leaving my children in the hands of Ruth." But I was so young—only nine years old. I cried.

As is still the custom in much of Africa today, mother's body was brought home to lie in state until the burial. There it was covered with sackcloth. I was so fearful, that I would only look through the window. I couldn't bring myself to actually go inside.

My older brother accused my father of having killed our mother. He said, "I told you to take her to the witch doctor because she had been cursed; but you refused.

You are responsible for her death. I hate you." Our father graciously said, "Son, I didn't kill your mother. She died in peace. You know she was born again."

At the burial site, father said, "Ruth, here is a piece of sackcloth. Because she has placed you responsible for the children, I want you to fold it and place it on your mother's head. When she is lowered into the ground, I want you to drop it in the ground with her." I cried so hard. I was so frightened and so very young.

CHAPTER 2 – Orphaned at Nine

After mother died we were taken out of school. Our father had to work, he couldn't tend the family garden nor did he have the money to pay our school fees. So he instructed us, "Children, you stay home and care for the garden and the goats while I go out and earn money for our food."

I remember in the mornings seeing neighborhood girls my age walk past our house, dressed nicely and well-fed on their way to school with their books. I cried because I wanted desperately to go to school.

Father finally became frustrated because of the hardship. When we would ask for anything he would slap us and say harshly, "Can't you see that I don't have money?" One day I determined that I was going to confront him. I waited for him to come home, and when he walked in I said, "Father, I want to go to school."

"What are you talking about?" he yelled. Can't you see that your older sisters and brothers aren't in school? Do you think that makes me happy? I've told you I don't have money for school fees. You must sit and wait."

"We have been waiting, father," I said.

"What is your suggestion?" he asked.

"Father," I said, "would you help me find a job?"

"Find *you* a job!? You're too young."

"But I'll try my best and work hard because I want to attend school," I said.

"Okay, I'll try," he promised. "I'll ask some of the nurses at the hospital if they will offer you a job."

That night, he returned home with a job for me. A

midwife (labor and delivery nurse) at the hospital had an 18-month-old son that I could take care of while she worked. He said, if you will take this job, I will use the money you earn to get you into school.

I was happy for several reasons. First, I wasn't going to have to dig in the garden with my siblings. Second, I wasn't going to have to go hungry. There would be food in the nurse's house. Third, I would have sugar for my tea. We were too poor to buy sugar for our tea. I knew the nurse, who had a baby, would also have sugar. And finally, I would earn the money necessary to get me back into school, where I longed to be.

The husband of the woman for whom I worked wouldn't give it to me. Instead, he gave it to my father. My father did allow me to enroll in school for which I was pleased.

On the other hand, I had no shoes or underpants. However, because my mother had assigned to me the responsibility for the family, they gave me her garment and shoes. Her shoes were too large for me so I stuffed them with paper and cloth. But they still didn't fit my tiny feet.

Father took my mother's garment to the local tailor who cut and sewed four dresses for me, all from the same material, which meant that all of my school dresses were the same color and pattern. Because of this, it appeared to my schoolmates that I never changed clothes. So the children made fun of me because I looked funny.

I wasn't being treated well working for the nurse. So both my job and my schooling were short lived. I was so disappointed. My siblings were happy to see me back home digging the garden with them.

After what seemed a long time, my father got me a job with another midwife. I worked for her family almost as a slave. Her husband was a rude drunkard who gave me difficult jobs that would have normally been done by adults.

One day her husband came home before his wife, and called me. He was quite drunk and angry as he grabbed me and began attempting to rape me. At that moment, he was interrupted by a knocked at the front door. I was so grateful. So, he pushed me out the back door, and as he did, he said, "Girl, don't you dare say anything to my wife or I will kill you. Do you understand me?" I was terrified.

One night I cooked a delicious sweet potato dinner in the outside kitchen. When I finished, I put the basket of food on my head to carry it into the big house where I would serve the family. *Note: in our part in the World this day, people carry large heavy loads balanced on their heads.* As I entered the big house I tripped and stumbled, the large basket fell to the ground and the sweet potatoes were scattered in the dust. My angry boss stormed out of the house shouting, "What have done you foolish girl?"

I explained, "I stumbled sir—it was an accident. I'm sorry, very sorry."

His wife would have nothing of it. She said, "You did this because you wanted to eat our food. Now you are going to do it. Eat all of the potatoes that you dropped!"

I cried and cried. But she shouted more loudly, "Eat them. Eat them all!"

She forced me to pick the dirt-covered sweet potatoes off the ground and put them in my mouth. It was nasty, horrible, and degrading. I chewed the grit-covered potatoes and swallowed them. That woman slapped the food out of my mouth and yelled: "Now you have eaten your salary. Tomorrow morning, pack your things and get out. Go!"

I didn't sleep at all that night. The next morning I took what little I had and slipped out of the house. I was fearful of returning to my own home because of what my father might say or do. I didn't know what to tell him. He was such a tough man.

I worked up the courage to go home and wait for my father to return from work. When he arrived, he walked in, saw me, and said: "What are you doing here? What's happened now? Do you have the money for school?"

I explained everything and told him I'd been fired.

"No more school for you," he said.

I cried. I was heartbroken.

My father found me another job as a baby sitter in the family of now retired Bishop Senabunlya of the Anglican Church at Namukozi. He and his family treated me well, God bless. The little money I earned there went to my father who was able to enroll me again in school, though it was very hard since my classmates would laugh at me.

Our father looked for families who would take us as foster-children. At times we were passed from family to family, which was quite difficult for us. Each family we lived with was different. It was hard to adjust. As a young girl I wanted to be loved, but no one showed me love, so I became bitter. I compared myself to other girls my age who were loved by their parents, whose needs were met; but I had nothing and no one.

One day a Muslim friend of my father dropped by the

house. He noticed the children and inquired of us. The man persuaded my father to allow him to take me to his house. He said, "I will take care of her, and pay for her schooling." My brothers and sisters were quite upset that I was being taken away.

When we arrived at his house I discovered another orphaned girl who was twelve years of age. The two of us slept together that night. The next morning the man came and explained that I was to attend the school near his house.

He said, "The food you eat while you're here with me, you will have to get on your own. Down the road is a boarding school. Each evening after they've fed their students dinner, you will go and collect scraps of food from their dining room. Those scraps will be what you will eat for lunch the next day.

"When you return from school, you must take my cattle out to graze until evening. You are to make sure they eat well. If I check them and discover that you've not fed them well, you will have no food either."

I was so scared, but since I had come to his house from my father's house at night, I didn't know how to get home. Remember, in those days we had no cell phones or Internet.

Day after day I dug in the man's garden and fetched his water, which often made me late for school, for which I was beaten.

One day, one of the male teachers stopped me and inquired as to why I was so sad, and why I was being beaten. I explained my situation and he said he could help me.

He lived near the road to school. He said that he

would leave his door unlocked and some books on his table. When I was going to be late for school, I could stop there and pick up the books and bring them with me to the school. When asked why I was late, I could explain that he had sent me to his house to get his books for him.

The next day, I did as he'd instructed. As I walked into his house to get the books as I had been told, there he stood in nothing but a towel around his waist. He closed the door behind me and raped me. I was devastated.

He said, "You must be quiet and tell no one what has happened. If you say anything at all, you will be killed. Don't tell anyone." I cried bitterly. He repeatedly raped me every day. When I complained he said, "I'm helping you stay in school. I'm protecting you from getting beaten. You should be grateful for my help." This continued through grades Primary 3 and Primary 4.

At night, the other orphaned girl there and I would go to the boarding school where we would wait in the dark until the students finished eating. Then like thieves, we would gather their leftovers and scraps, and carry the saucepans on our heads.

By the time lunch rolled around the next day, the food we had collected from the garbage was often unfit to eat, but we ate it anyway because it was the only food we had. And with the blood thirsty Idi Amin in power, (Uganda's third president who some report killed as many as 12 million people) we had no sugar. So we'd sweeten our tea with a piece of raw sugar cane. I suffered. I had no soap to wash my uniform so I would get pawpaw leaves and put them in water, squeeze them then wash my clothes. (Pawpaws are a type of fruit.)

Taking care of the cattle wasn't easy. I had to lead them into the bush, whether it was sunny or rainy, and bring them back well fed so they could be checked. Some nights I was denied dinner because the Muslim man said I hadn't fed them well.

One day my father came to visit me. I told him how unhappy I was. He said, "Ruth, I'm going to talk with the pastor of the Full Gospel Church and see if he can help you."

The pastor told him, "Bring Ruth here and I will look after her." Here is what I later learned.

When my mother died 14 days after giving birth, Florence, my baby sister stayed at the hospital because my father was incapable of caring for her. When she was six months old, the pastor asked my father if he and his wife, who had no children, could adopt Florence. My father was happy to know that they would lovingly care for his baby girl.

That pastor's family picked me up from the Muslim man's home and took me home with them. They asked that I not tell Florence, my little sister, now their daughter, that she had been adopted. "The day you reveal to Florence that she isn't our own daughter, you must leave our house," they said. The pastor paid my Primary 5 school fees, and at 13 years of age I was back in school. Sadly, I was seriously abused in the pastor's home as well, but I could tell no one. NOTE: In some African countries women are generally culturally disregarded, even abused by some men who appear respectable in society.

In that home we use to wake up at 5:00 a.m. to dig the garden before school. Waking up that early was so hard that I would sometimes skip dinner and tell them I was sick (when I wasn't) so they wouldn't wake me up to dig.

CHAPTER 3 – Pregnant At Fifteen

Before I completed Primary 7, at age 15, I discovered that I was pregnant. The father of the child was a large Muslim man who often drove through the neighborhood in a big black car, which I thought was a Mercedes Benz. I assumed he was a famous movie star or someone very important. He stopped when he saw me on the street and invited me to get into his car. He told me he loved me. No one had ever loved me. I was so excited to be loved.

After being with him many times, one night the pastor caught me getting into the man's car. I was chased away, I couldn't go with the Muslim man because I'd recently discovered that he had three wives, and I refused to be his fourth. Every adult I knew rejected me because I had conceived at such a young age.

I couldn't return to my father, he had no place for me. Instead, I went to one of my sisters and told her my story. I asked if I could stay with her. She said she was sorry to hear all I that had been through, but that she and her boyfriend lived there in one room and they had no place for me. She sent me into the village. Village life was quite difficult.

One day in the village I met a man who had come from Kamapala City to bury his father. When we met, he offered to take me to Kampala with him. Once in Kampala he used me for some time, along with other ladies who came and went. I was so desperate for love that I continued to allow a victim mentality to control me. I didn't know any different.

I remembered a lady I had known when I was but a

child. She lived about four miles from where I was staying. I went to see if she could offer me any help. She explained that she had no room for me, but suggested that I go back to the pastor and his wife and repent to them. She explained that since I was pregnant, I needed to be near the Muslim man who had fathered my child so he could take care of me. So I returned to the pastor's home.

They allowed me to sleep in the room next to their kitchen. But I was to live separately and provide my own food. The Muslim man was hardly supportive. He told me that I should move in and be his fourth wife, otherwise he wouldn't feed me. My womb was growing and I had almost no clothing that would fit. The people in the church laughed at and mocked me. "Young girl, why are you pregnant?"

Six months into my pregnancy I asked a neighbor girl to inquire of her mother what it was like to give birth. She returned saying, "Mother said that you will feel pain all over your womb then the nurse will tell you to push the baby out." That was all the prenatal instruction I was given.

Sure enough the time came when I had pain all over my womb. I ran to the pastor and his wife and told them. They said, "We are sorry, but there is no fuel. We'll have to push you to the hospital in a wheelbarrow. As they put me into the wheelbarrow, a boy appeared on a bicycle. They stopped him and asked him to take me to the hospital on his bicycle, which he did. They left me with the boy, who dropped me off at the hospital, all alone.

My first midwife was a tough woman with no

patience with me at all. She didn't want to hear anything I had to say. She instructed me to go lie down on a bed. I did.

When I cried out in pain, as a woman does in childbirth, she yelled, "Shut up! If you don't keep your mouth closed, that child will come out of your mouth!" No one had told me that it would be so painful. I was sweating and in agony. I went to the receptionist for some comfort. When she saw me, she yelled, "Go get back in bed and shut your mouth!" Afterwards she came and checked me.

Then she said, "Now push!" I had been waiting for that. The baby was born, but not without complications. Due to the pushing and the lack of proper medical care I received, I had physical problems

My step-mother in the village came to assist me since I couldn't walk or sit because I required eight stitches from giving birth. As was the custom in Uganda at the time, the Muslim man who had fathered my child bought one kilo of cow intestines for my people to cook into a soup for me to eat so I could breastfeed my baby daughter. The man gave me very little support. It took me a longer time to recover than normal due to the lack of prenatal care and the careless way I was treated during delivery.

When my daughter was four months old, she was sickly and had no clothes. I was advised to go to her father and get help, even clothing for myself. I still looked terrible, and the harsh life I was living made matters even worse.

So I visited his shop in town and told him that our child was very sick. I explained that she needed to go to the hospital, but I had no money. I explained how she had nothing, no clothing or even a blanket in which to sleep at night. When I finished, he said: "I told you I loved YOU, not a child. If you want anything from me you must sleep with me again. Then, and only then, will I support your child." For fear of getting pregnant again, I took my sick child and walked out crying.

Uganda under Idi Amin's ruthless rule was a place of incomprehensible misery. There was no freedom of worship. Amin had closed the churches, and tortured and killed Christians, many of whom were hiding in the forests and underground in fear for their lives. Hundreds of pastors were arrested, and none were allowed to pray openly. We were young, but we saw how people struggled.

Life was difficult. I had no money, no job, and a baby to support. I began to look for other men so I could feed her. My pain and guilt drove me to drink. I was miserable.

I began to frequent bars looking for money to buy her milk and clothes. Some of my friends suggested that I visit a witch doctor so he could "witch my child's father" into giving us help.

When my baby was seven months old I went into a bar, I had a wealthy male friend who was married. He and his wife often came into that bar, and he would occasionally give me money to feed my daughter. In fact, he had told the bar owner that whenever I came into the bar, he was to treat me very well. He was to give me free beer and drinks, and charge them to his account.

That night he came with his wife. He shared a table

with a district commissioner. When closing time came, he asked his friend to take me home.

As we got into the car, an army lieutenant also climbed in. As we drove toward my neighborhood, the lieutenant pulled a gun on the commissioner and ordered him not to slow down. He wasn't stopping at all. I shouted, "This is where I live! Please stop and let me out!"

The man yelled back angrily, "Don't talk!" He poked the driver with his pistol and said, "Don't stop!" They continued on to the army barracks in a place called Buye. In my mind I decided that when they arrived at the barracks, I would simply refuse to leave the car.

Sure enough, when the car stopped at the barracks he climbed out and commanded me to get out of the car. I refused. He yelled, but I refused. With that, he pulled his gun and hit me across the face with it. I felt warm blood running down my cheek. He took me from the car and dragged me inside the barracks. I was familiar with the barracks, because I once had a boyfriend who lived there. My friend Joyce was a cook there.

"What have you done?" I asked. "You are a friend of my friend."

"Don't tell anyone," he said. I knew he planned to rape me.

Then he went into the bathroom and began to vomit. I got up and peeked. The sink was full of blood. He was vomiting blood. Slowly and quietly I crept to the door, opened it quietly, stepped outside, and ran as fast as I could. I ran to Joyce's house in the barracks. .

She came to the door and asked what I was doing there. I said, "Allow me to come in and I will tell you."

Joyce opened the door and I rushed in. I told her

everything. She said, "Do you realize what you've done to me? If that man finds out that I've assisted you, he will have me killed. Everybody fears him. I only have one room." I begged her to hide me under her bed and cover me with a cloth. She did.

She watched for him the next morning. When he left for town, I ran to my village. When I returned to the bar, I told my boyfriend what his friend, the district lieutenant had done. He confronted him. The man said, "I was drunk and not thinking clearly. But, she escaped. So I didn't do anything at all to her."

A few nights later as I walked home from the bar, that same lieutenant passed me in his car. He stopped, and he was drunk. He climbed out and began to chase me. I ran into a banana plantation with him on my heels. He slipped and fell into a ditch. With that, I ran back to the bar and beat on the door. The bar keeper said I should stop coming there, because the man would continue to find me.

When my daughter was nine months, I met another man who told me he was a pilot. I was excited. I thought, *"This man will provide a good life for me and my daughter."* I left my daughter in the home of the pastor and his wife, and went to live with that man. Before long, I learned that he could neither read nor write. He was totally uneducated, and certainly not a pilot. Though he had lied to me, I stayed with him.

Later I conceived my second child, and life was even more difficult. The worst part was that he was harsh and demanding, engaged in witchcraft, and wouldn't allow me to visit my first-born daughter at the pastor's house. One day I found nine pairs of underwear tied together. I learned that it was a form of witchcraft. He admitted that he wore all of them to gain riches, and that they were not to ever be washed.

He was also quite a womanizer. When it was time for me to give birth I asked him for money to buy clothes because the hospital always asks, "What will you be wearing home?"

He said, "I'm not going to give you any money for clothing for a child I've never seen. When the baby is born, I'll come and buy the clothes."

I went secretly to his business, opened his safe, and took out the money I needed for clothing for our child. Then I went out and purchased them. When I returned I put the receipts on the bed so he'd know that I had bought only children's clothing. When he came back that night, he looked, saw the receipts and the missing money, and became enraged.

I was in the kitchen when he called for me. When I walked into the bedroom, he locked the door and began to interrogate me. He wanted to know where I got the money for the purchases. He opened the safe and when he saw the money was missing he was livid. He shook me, and yelled, "Who told you that you could take my money?"

I replied, "I used it to buy clothing for our child."

"You know you aren't allowed to touch my money," he screamed as he threw me out of the house at night, pregnant and almost due.

I walked alone in the darkness. I remembered a midwife who lived nearby. So, I stopped at her house to see if she would help me.

"Who is it?" she asked.

"It is Ruth," I answered.

"Are you alone?" She asked.

I explained how and why my husband had discarded me. She opened the door and took me in. She found it hard to believe that the father of my child would treat me that way when I was so close to giving birth.

Two days later my second child was born. The midwife immediately went to get the baby's father. Although he wanted nothing to do with me or our baby, he brought the suitcase full of baby clothes that I had purchased and gave them to us. My child and I stayed with her for the first week, after which we moved back into his house. It was horrible. He mistreated me as he caroused with his other girlfriends. The witchcraft in his room was almost palpable—simply too much for me to bear.

After a few days, my younger brother came by to check on me. When he saw the deplorable circumstances under which I was living he said, "Ruth, tomorrow when this man leaves for work, I will come and get you and your daughter and take you back to our village."

He did, and when we arrived at the village I moved into my father's house with my daughter. Not only was he a poor man, who had nothing. But his house was already full of children. He truly had no room for us.

A few days later, the vengeful father of my child came to the door with a policeman, accused me of robbing him, and claimed that I was not his wife. The policeman demanded that I return everything I had "stolen." They took me the police station together with my innocent father. So I handed him the suitcase and the child's father demanded that I also return the pants I was wearing. All my poor father could do was stand there and weep.

One day I went to visit the family with whom I had left my first-born, Swas, who was now almost a year old. They lived deep in the village. When I arrived, she didn't recognize me. And I could see that she was quite ill. I asked permission to take her back, because there was no medical help available where they lived.

Now I was a single mother of two. I decided to go back where I left my first born and beg them for a place to stay. They accepted me on the condition that I feed myself. They said they were responsible only for my first born whom I had left with them at the age of nine months. I was given a small room next to their kitchen, it was terrible. As they cooked the smoke from the burning firewood would fill my room. The Muslim father of my second born would drop by from time to time and demand to take his daughter. He would ask me to come live with him, but I told him that I would never live with him again. Then one day he came and took our daughter. I had no choice he took her back to his family. There was nothing I could do.

CHAPTER 4 – Prostitution

By this time I didn't know what to do. I had been used, abused, and dumped by several men. At that point I decided to go to Villa Maria in Masaka District, which was about 150 miles from my home Mityana. Because of bad roads, it was a long arduous journey. I knew a nurse there who worked in Kiyinda Hospital. She was a longtime friend who had returned to care for her dying father in Masaka. Earlier, she'd given me directions to his home in case I ever needed her, so I headed to Masaka to find her.

When I arrived she was pleased to see me, but the situation wasn't good. Each morning we would dig in the vegetable garden.

One day her brother came to visit her. He asked who I was. She said, "Ruth is my friend who has come to see me. I've taken her as my sister."

He said, "If she is your sister, then she is my sister too."

"Come sister, and allow me to show you Masaka. I'll give you a tour of the city and introduce you to my wife and family as well..

It sounded good. When we reached Nyendo trading center, near Masaka, I met a young girl who I recognized. She and her family were from my home village. I knew her family very well.

I asked what she was doing in Nyendo, and she asked me the same. I explained my situation to her and she said, "Oh, go back and get your bags. You can stay with me and learn what I do to earn money. You can earn money here to send back home to care for your children. I agreed. I had always wanted to provide for my children.

As promised, my friend's brother took me to meet his family, then returned me to his sister's home. As soon as we arrived, I got my bag and he escorted me to the young lady's house in Nyendo.

When I arrived, she took me to the room where I was to stay. To my shock, there were six other girls in that one small room. I asked her, "What are you doing? How do you earn money here? What is the job are you offering me?"

She said, "My five friends and I work together. We sleep here in the day, and we work at night. We will teach you how we earn money."

I was anxious to hear about the job, but they told me nothing more until that evening. We showered and dressed together, but I had nothing nice to wear. One of the girls, my age and size, allowed me to borrow some of her clothes; gave me cream and makeup, and brushed my hair nicely.

Around 8:00 p.m. we left and went to a bar. As we walked in and sat down, my friend explained, "Ruth, what we do is sit here and wait for men. When they walk in, if one of them wants you, you must go with him, please him, and in the morning he will give you some money. That's what we do.

It's important that you do not spend all of the money, because you'll need it the next night to buy beer and wait for other men."

It didn't seem like hard work, and it appeared that I could earn a lot of money. At the beginning in my naiveté I didn't realize I was entering a life of prostitution.

I soon learned that it wasn't nearly as easy as they'd promised. Some men hurt me, others wouldn't pay what they'd promised. But I stayed because I felt I had no other options.

The lady who owned the bar seemed to love me. She would support me and compliment me to the men. I welcomed her attention, and would even share my money with her at times, but I didn't realize at the time that she was doing it to sell more beer to the men.

CHAPTER 5 – SERIOUS RELATIONSHIP

One day a man came in and told me he wanted to take me out of the bar, out of prostitution. He asked me to marry him and help him set up a shop. I shared that information with the bar owner who said, "Ruth, this is wonderful news. Let's look for a shop." So we did.

We found a shop in Kirimya. When he returned from Kampala City that night we told him that we had a place. He gave us the money to get the shop. My friend, who had helped me find the shop, suggested that we begin with bananas and pineapples. "Later," she explained, "you can add more products, like sugar to sell." To our surprise, the new business expanded and I was able to buy sugar in large bags and sell it in smaller quantities. Business was good! That meant that our relationship had ended, but I was happy. I owned a business.

In 1982 I received the bad news that my father back home in the village had fallen on a bicycle and had broken two ribs. He was admitted into Mulago hospital in Mityana my home District. During that time, war had broken out and there were military road blocks everywhere.

At the road blocks, soldiers would drag people from their cars, beat, rape, and even kill them. Traveling was quite difficult.

I put on a modest traditional dress that covered everything, and a scarf on my head, and left to go home and see my father. I was able to make my way through each of the roadblocks to reach my father's house. I had taken personal items and bed sheets so that he could be cared for properly at the hospital, but when I arrived, he had been dismissed and was at home. Since he was doing better, after three days with him, I returned to Kirimya.

There I boarded a taxi to Kampala City, where I changed and took another a taxi to Masaka. I climbed into the back seat of the taxi and sat down by Kisekka, a young man I knew from Masaka. We talked and I asked him why he had come to Mityana. He explained that he had come to get a passport. We chatted until we came to a horrible roadblock at Nsangi. That roadblock was well known nation-wide as a terrible place to pass. The man in charge of the roadblock was an evil soldier named Sokolo, an army Captain. He was a killer, rapist, and kidnapper. People cringed at the mention of his name.

We were stopped and commanded to exit the taxi. I was in the back seat, so I was the last to climb out of the car. He checked Kisekka's ID and allowed him to get in the car. Then he came to me.

He looked at me and said, "You. You are a prostitute."

I said, "No. I'm not a prostitute."

With that, he asked for my ID. I gave it to him. He looked at it and back at me, and said, "Do you have any other possessions in the car?"

I told him my bag was in the car.

He had the driver take my bag from the car and put my ID in his pocket.

When the driver returned with my bag, Sokolo asked me, "Do you know anyone else in that taxi?"

I said, "Yes. I know the man who was seated with me on the back seat."

He commanded that Kisekka be taken from the car

and brought to him.

By that time, Sokolo was infuriated. He was a very black man and his eyes were now red with anger. He screamed at the driver, "Go! Get out of here." The taxi tires screeched as the driver fled the roadblock.

As our taxi left, he commanded Kisekka and me to sit and wait across the road. There was only a broken chair in which to sit. As we did, Captain Sokolo continued to check other cars.

Suddenly, a Matatu drove up. It was similar to a van in the U.S. except that the two rear seats faced each other. He told two of his soldiers to get Kisekka and me, and my bag, and put us in the vehicle. They drove us to the Mpigi Military Barracks, which are off the main road.

As they pulled up to the Captain's living quarters they commanded us to get out and sit on the veranda. When they left, Kisekka said, "Ruth, what have you done to me? Why did you mention my name? They are now going to kill me. They'll rape you and perhaps allow you to live. But I'm as good as dead."

I explained that when the Captain asked me if I knew anyone else in the car, I had mentioned him, because I had felt that it would help me escape. I had no idea that I would be putting him in such a bad situation.

Captain Sokolo was in the house for two hours while we sat waiting outside. Looking back now I suspect that he must have been taking drugs.

When he returned his eyes were still red and continued interrogating me. "You are a prostitute If not, then where is your husband?"

I can't explain how I had the awareness to do so, but I remembered another army Captain that I had fallen in love with when I worked in the bar. I mentioned him by name and said, "He is my husband."

Sokolo challenged, "Okay, if he is your husband, let him come here now and get you."

He accused Kisekka of being a rebel. When he opened his case and found his passport papers, he said, "Now I have you! This passport is for your attempt to run away, you rebel."

"Woman," he said to me, "I'm not allowing you to leave until the Captain you've mentioned comes to get you."

With that, he returned inside the barracks for another two hours, after which he came back outside to the veranda, looked at me with those red eyes, and asked: "Do you think I will allow you to leave?"

"I don't know," I replied fearfully.

With that he went back into the barracks and left me outside until it was almost dark. When he returned, he threw my ID card in my lap and barked, "Have we done anything to hurt you!?"

"No sir," I replied.

"Did we rob you?" He asked.

"No you haven't, sir," I said.

"If we let you go will you be able to get to where you are going?" He asked.

I said, "Yes." Then at that precise moment I heard a bus approaching, on its way to the village.

He said, "Here comes a bus now, take your things and go!"

Kisekka and I ran out and flagged down the bus. But when the door opened, there was no place to sit. Even the aisle was filled with people. So, we crammed ourselves inside and sat on the steps, with the door open until the bus got to the main highway.

At the highway we got off of the bus. I was too shaky to walk. Kisekka fussed at me about the trouble I'd caused him. "You could've gotten me killed," he kept saying.

It was very dark when an empty lorry (truck) pulled up, on its way to Masaka to pick up a load of bananas. We stopped it and I begged the driver to let us ride. I couldn't get on the truck, so Kisekka and the driver virtually threw me aboard. The truck then continued down the pothole filled highway. The ride was rugged, and by the time we arrived in Nyendo it was quite dark. When I got off the truck I was in such pain I could barely walk, and hardly carry my bag. I finally made it to my house and knew that it was a miracle that we'd escaped. It was certainly an act of God. I continued to run my small shop selling bananas, pineapples, and sugar. By 1984 my shop was doing quite well, when a friend of mine suggested that I could do even better if I would sell beer and cigarettes, so I agreed.

One day a kind man came into the shop to buy something. He and I struck up a conversation. He returned several times and we became friends. He worked in Kampala City and would come to see me every weekend. One day I asked if he was married. He said that he wasn't. I was so happy. Eventually, he introduced me to his family.

In 1986, when the revolution in Uganda occurred and the government was overthrown, soldiers from Tanzania passed through our town on their way to Kampala. Even when the road from our village to Kampala was blocked because of the war, he would go through Kenya and Tanzania to get to me.

War was ugly. People were dying everywhere. He took me to his family where we stayed for some time. Then I returned to my shop.

The soldiers liked my shop because I sold beer and cigarettes. They not only bought things from me, they guarded my shop. When my supplies ran low, they would even escort me to go buy more. When the fighting grew worse we were forced to leave and hide out in Kirimya.

When the new president took power, the roadblocks were fewer and the soldiers departed. Once again we were able to go to town and buy the things we needed.

This man with whom I was living said, "Ruth, I want to buy you some land and build a home for you so you can be my wife in Masaka."

Then one day a woman from Kampala City came looking for him. That's when I discovered that he was married. When he came home I told him that he'd lied to me. He said, "Don't worry about it. She lives in Kampala and has everything she needs. You are here in Masaka, and I will see to it that you also have everything you need." So, I was content.

I found 10 acres of land, and he gave me the money with which to purchase it. Later I found five more close by. I hired people to break up the soil and plant a big banana plantation. Later I bought other 20 acres with money he gave me. We built a big mansion and he furnished it well. "Ruth, this will be your home," he said.

I was happy. He loved and supported me. I was able to go back and get my two daughters and bring them to live with me there. Then I conceived.

When I gave birth to my daughter, my third born, he treated all of us well. He paid the workers and they treated us well.

CHAPTER 6 – Saved!

In 1989 Pastor Musoke, who is in heaven now, came to me. He was a friend who would come to my shop for supplies. I sold him sugar and soap. Sometimes I just give him what he needed to help his family because they had little money. He told me, "I have invited some friends of mine in Kampala City to Masaka to conduct a crusade."

Then one day a truck came through town with loud speakers announcing the crusade, which was to begin on Monday. The loud speakers were so loud that I could hear the music and the messages from my shop.

I couldn't help but notice that those who participated in the crusade looked underfed and weren't very well dressed. On Wednesday I confronted the pastor and said, "Pastor, will you allow me to cook a dinner for your guests?"

He said, "Of course. That would be wonderful." So I did. I cooked chicken, meat, and matooke (a main dish made from mashed steamed bananas). My maid delivered the food to the crusade team. When she returned the next morning to pick up our dishes everything was empty.

On Thursday, as the services began on the fourth day of the crusade, I asked my maid to watch the shop so I could visit the crusade. I wanted to see if everything was well. Sure enough, the crusade team had devoured the food.

I stood at a distance in the back of the crowd because I didn't want to mix with the group. The visiting preacher preached a powerful Gospel sermon from Matthew 11:28. He said that Jesus had said, *"Come unto me all you who labor and are heavy laden, and I will give you rest."*

Rest? Could anyone give me rest? I thought. *My husband is rich, he owns several companies, and has many women. But I had no rest. Me? I consult with witches and witch doctors to get him to love me; because I want him to be with me alone. I seldom sleep well.* I wondered, *can anyone love me and give me peace?*

I didn't turn to go back to my shop. I just wanted to hear what else the preacher had to say. Then in that moment the preacher said, "Come to Jesus and He will give you peace. Is there anyone here who wants to surrender his or her life to Jesus? Only Jesus can give you true peace and rest for your soul. It's free. If so, please raise your hand so I can pray with you."

I raised my hand and everyone looked at me. After all, I was a rich man's wife, the shop owner. I was rather famous in that area. People could hardly believe their eyes that I had raised my hand.

A man standing near me said, "Ruth, did you hear clearly what the preacher just said? He's inviting you to receive Christ into your life." I assured him that I did understand.

Then the preacher invited each of us who had raised our hands to join him at the front and pray with him. I didn't walk, *I ran to the front!*

The people were shocked. They knew me. They knew my shop, where I sold the beer and cigarettes.

Is it true? Is she really going to the front to receive Christ? They must have thought.

With both hands up, I sincerely repeated the words that the preacher led us to pray. And the moment I said the words, "I confess Jesus as my personal Savior," for the first time in my life, my heart was flooded with true peace."

It was getting dark as I returned to my shop. But I didn't hesitate. I opened the fridge and began to throw out the beer and cigarettes, my two top grossing products. People said, "Ruth has gone mad. We don't know what those 'Christians' have done to her, but they have driven her mad!"

I told them, "I will no longer sell beer and cigarettes. I am a saved woman!"

My husband was on business in Nairobi, Kenya, our neighboring country. I called him from our home phone and told him, "Honey, I have good news. I am saved. People came to preach and I gave my life to Jesus. I'm no longer selling beer and cigarettes, I'm a new person!"

"What are you talking about," he asked, "we are Catholics. We don't 'get saved.' I didn't know that you were a sinner, and that I was living with a sinful woman."

"Yes, I was a sinner," I replied, "but now I am saved."

With that, he hung up on me, and I cried. I thought, *now my husband is going to return and chase me away because I'm saved. What shall I do?*

I ran to the pastor who encouraged and prayed for me and my husband.

When my husband returned home I did my best to explain to him what had happened in my heart. He listened quietly. I continued to live with him and to pray for his salvation. He used to come and ask me to send my maid to the nearest bar to buy him beers, by that time I could not, and feel good. I grew to hate the smell of beer. But I had nothing to do. I was praying for him to receive what I had received.

CHAPTER 7 – Widowed

The last week of July in 1991, my husband returned to town and came to the house. It was a Saturday and he wasn't feeling well. His stomach was hurting and he asked me to pray for him, which I did.

Looking back now, I remember seeing him with a packet of drugs called "PCM," a drug to treat HIV/AIDS patients that only the rich could buy. It had to be purchased in Nairobi, Kenya. When I had asked about it he explained that it was for his elder brother who was sick by that time.

On Monday he delivered a load of bananas to Kampala City. On Tuesday he told me that he was quite sick. Then on Wednesday one of his truck drivers told me that I should come to Kampala City for he was seriously ill, and had been admitted into Kampala's Mulago hospital.

I went to one of my friends and asked her if she would accompany me to Kamala to check on him. As we neared the city and came to the Kibuye round-about, we heard an announcement on the taxi's radio. The announcer said that my husband was dead! I couldn't believe it. She held me.

We immediately hired a car and went to his house in Kampala. Once there we were told that his body had been taken to our home in Masaka. So my friend and I returned home. It was there that many other women, along with children that he had fathered, came to pay their respect. He had at least ten children from six different women.

The following day, we went to bury him in his village. I was confused. My husband had died, without ever coming to know Christ as his Savior, or even entering our new home. We had planned to move into our mansion in September and he died in August. I was in shock.

I returned to my shop and at the end of the first month, his sister came with her children and took over my house. After a few days she told me in no uncertain terms that I was no longer welcome in that home, and that my deceased husband's family would no longer support me.

By then, because of all of my troubles I had lost interest in my shop, which was no longer producing a livable wage. My husband died in August and September through December were three horrible months. I was a rejected widow who had lost her home and all of her property. I had no job, and was left with three children to support. I had no family because my mother had died when I was nine-years-old; and by then, my father was also deceased. I was given no voice in the matter.

My newly deceased husband's family was the only family I knew. In fact, my mother-in-law had become more like a mother to me. But with her son's death, she actually accused me of killing him; and she and the family took everything he and I owned, and deserted me. They treated like a stranger. In the process, I lost my reputation, my friends, my confidence and even my health. I resorted to begging for food.

It was in that condition that a dear friend of mine asked me if I knew what had killed my husband. I told her that I didn't know, but that his illness was rather short. She told me that my husband had had a Tanzanian girlfriend who had died of AIDS. I remembered how I'd discovered that my husband had hidden the fact that he too was taking strong drugs. Now he was gone and my children and I had nothing.

When the third sister in my family had died of AIDS, my other siblings offered to come and assist me. However, I knew that were that to happen, I would be expected to pay their round trip transportation, which I could no longer do. Although I wanted their assistance, I discouraged them from coming.

In Western countries widows are cared for by their families, their friends, churches and social agencies. However, in Uganda, a widow is considered an outcast, in some cases when a man dies his widow is forced to marry one of his brothers, and that's how HIV/AIDS was spread. It was much worse in those days. Realizing that my husband had died of AIDS, I wondered if I too might have contracted the deadly disease. I was becoming increasingly sickly and weak. There was no one to take me to the hospital and I had no money for food or medication. One night my youngest daughter then only 4 years old, awoke in the night and cried because she was hungry. I grieved.

The district in which we lived was Uganda's most AIDS-ravaged. One day my brother-in-law came to see us and asked me if I would accept him as a replacement for his deceased brother so that he could care for us. He was a Muslim with three wives. I refused him and told him about my Christian faith. He said, "Then you will receive nothing from us." He stood and walked out.

One morning I woke up and determined that I would go to him and ask to rent one of his many houses in Kampala City, and if he could help me move there. He agreed, but said that when the truck came to get me I would have to purchase the fuel for the move. Interestingly, the truck was one that my husband had owned. So I collected enough money from my friends to move to his two-bedroom house, and in 1992 we moved to Zana, outside of Kampala.

It was quite a challenge with my three children and my three-year-old sister that my deceased father had left me to care for in his will. So my four children, my maid who had been with me for several years, and I moved into the two bedroom house.

One day my maid said, "Mama, we don't have enough food for the six of us. Let me go and try to find my own way." It was painful to release her, but I didn't have the money to keep her.

I struggled to keep the four children in school. At one point I asked my brother-in-law for a little money to start a business so I could support my family. He loaned me a small amount with which I bought and resold maize (corn), but the business didn't work. Because my husband had owned a big spare auto parts business, I went to my brother-in-law and asked him to give me a few auto parts which I could sell. By then, he and his family had sold our houses and cars.

One day my Bishop's wife called and suggested that I allow her to help me see a lawyer so I could recover something for my children. I had no money for a lawyer.

CHAPTER 8 – AIDS

In 1992 I had returned to Kampala and began suffering the terrible symptoms of AIDS. I had:
- Debilitating headaches,
- Diarrhea,
- Loss of appetite with extreme weight loss,
- Vomiting,
- Fever, with shivering all night, and
- Was in constant pain.

I felt for certain that I was dying of AIDS as had my husband and his girlfriend. I had all the symptoms, but I had no money to go to the hospital.

My neighbor, also a widow, asked me one day, "Ruth, why are you dying at home. Why don't you go to the hospital?"

I explained to her that I could afford neither hospitalization nor medication.

She was so kind. She took me to her family doctor for treatment, and she covered the costs.

I was so encouraged to see her doctor. For eight months her doctor treated me with tablets and injections. Even so, I was not getting better.

On January 16, 1993 the situation grew critical. I called my two daughters who were then seventeen- and eighteen-years-old, and I asked them to transport me to the hospital. By then I couldn't even get to and from the toilet without assistance. I was dying, and didn't want to die in their prese6nce. I asked that they drop me off at the hospital. So they came and carried me to the car because I was too weak to walk.

As we neared the hospital I said, "Girls, let's change plans. Take me first to my doctor who gives me tablets and injections. Perhaps she has a recommendation for me."

So they took me to see her. When she saw me she was shocked, and asked if I was dying. She thought I had stopped talking my medication. I assured her that I was still taking it, but it wasn't helping. Since there was no improvement, she insisted that I allow her to test my blood for HIV/AIDS.

"Go ahead and test my blood," I said. "But do it quickly. I'm running out of time." she tested my blood and told me to return in seven days.

A week later, I returned to hear the awful news that like my husband who had died, I too was HIV positive. Though devastated, I reluctantly accepted the news, but wondered what would happen to my girls.

The doctor told me that if I expected to live to take care of my girls, I would have to eat well, abstain from sex, and continue to come to her for medication.

"Doctor," I explained. "I can't eat at all. Whatever I eat comes right back up. My husband is dead, so abstaining from sex is no problem. I'm a saved Christian. Please allow me to return home where I can pray, repent to the Lord, and ask Him to heal me."

The doctor felt it was unwise, but relented. My daughters placed me in the car and on our way home I asked them to take me by the church. We found four women at the church, the *Prayer Palace Christian Center*. They prayed a brief prayer for me. Then my daughters took me home.

Once home, I went into my room and placed my

doctor's written diagnosis that said that I was HIV positive on the bed. I knelt, I wept, and I prayed. I didn't blame my dead husband for anything. I took responsibility for myself, and the result of my choices.

I prayed, "Lord, I have been given a bad report. But you've said in Luke 18:27 that things that are impossible with men are possible with you. My being healed of the AIDS virus is impossible with men but with you all things are possible

You said in Jeremiah 32:27 that you are *"the God of all flesh, and nothing is too hard for you."* I quoted 2 Chronicles 7:14 and reminded Him that He had said *if we'd pray and seek His face, repent and turn from our wicked ways that He would heal our land.* I said, "Lord I have done that. Heal me and I will tell all the people that You are the Healer of AIDS."

CHAPTER 9 – Healed

I said, "Lord, you give men who make automobiles the wisdom to make spare parts for them, knowing that there will come a day when the car will break down and need them. You created me and all of the organs in my body. I need my spare parts today, Lord. Heal me and transform me that I may see my children's children."

After I finished praying I fell asleep.

At midnight I began sweating profusely. I thought I was dying. I had watched others die of AIDS, and knew that sweating was part of it. I didn't know that God was intervening. I didn't know that He had heard my desperate prayer and that His hand was at work.

My worst symptom of all was the excruciatingly painful headaches. But when I awoke the next morning, the terrible headaches were gone. I supposed that they would return. But after a whole day, they didn't. Nor did they return the second day. However, the other symptoms remained. But because my headaches were gone, I had faith to believe that the other symptoms would go as well. So much so, that I began to speak to those symptoms. I told them about God's faithfulness to me and announced to them that they were leaving also.

In 1993 God began to gradually heal me. Day by day over the course of that year my strength returned and my symptoms left. It took an entire year. That year I fell in love with Jesus in fresh new ways. I wanted to be with Him.

In May of 1994 it was announced that *Prayer Palace Christian Center's* senior pastor, his wife and eight children who had preached the gospel when I was born again, was returning to Uganda from five years living in Canada. He was returning to pray for the healing of our nation.

I was overjoyed to hear he was coming. Our church organized a group to go and pick him up from the airport. Another group remained at the church to prepare for his arrival. He looked so good as he walked to the pulpit where he explained that he had returned to Uganda as a result of a vision God had given him on a visit to the United States. It was a vision of a pregnant woman. Everything in her was rotten. There was no hope for her. God told him that his nation, Uganda, was hopelessly sick and that He (God) was Uganda's only hope. God said, "Go tell her to come back to me. I'm going to heal Uganda."

We are going to war against the terrible killer, AIDS, in Uganda through prayer and fasting. God is going to hear His children and heal our land. He announced that we would fast and pray for 40 days. In addition, the church paid for radio announcements to call people to fast and pray. People were invited to come and spend time at the church praying and fasting. And those who were sick were invited to come by for prayer.

People came from many different churches. Many people were brought in wheel barrows near the gates of the church. The church was like a hospital. People with many different sicknesses and symptoms came for prayer.

The praying people were like soldiers of Christ to fight the sickness and ravages of AIDS. God was hearing and answering our prayers. Newspaper reporters wrote articles about what God was doing, and of course there were some who mocked what we were doing. There always is.

Some criticized us saying, "Some of those sick people are likely to die at your church." The pastor explained that people also die at hospitals, but they aren't prevented from going there. "How can I tell the sick that they cannot come to the church for prayer?" He asked.

Some, like me, were fasting all day for 12 hours, and then we would eat a light dinner. But others, like our pastor, were not eating solid food at all began to look in poor health after many days. He lost lots of weight.

When the 40 days of prayer and fasting concluded I went to my pastor and asked what I should do. He told me to return to my doctor for a checkup. I did.

My doctor was amazed to see me alive. After all, she had managed my medical file and treated me for eight months. She drew blood and tested it. A week later, I returned to hear her declare that I was 100% HIV Negative! I was healed!

I asked, "Doctor, can you explain this?"

She assured me that she couldn't. "There is nothing in your blood, Ruth."

I explained to her about the power of prayer and fasting and God's faithfulness to keep His word. Then I returned to the church with my HIV negative report.

The pastor said, "This is wonderful, Ruth. Please come back and give a testimony to the people of God's faithfulness and your healing." I assured him I would.

That night I returned and testified. God blessed my testimony and those who heard it. From that time forward, God began to heal those who trusted Him.

Among them, a policeman and a policewoman were both healed of AIDS. My testimony appeared in the newspaper every day with the church's phone number to call for healing.

One day an army lieutenant called the church and asked to speak to the pastor. The young man who answered the phone explained that the pastor wasn't in. He said, "I have AIDS and I wanted the pastor to pray for me." The young man said, "I will pray for you." As the boy prayed, the man's open sores closed and crusted over. The following day the officer went to the military hospital to be tested. He too was totally healed of AIDS.

In December, the Ugandan AIDS Commissioner sent a letter saying he had heard rumors of what was happening as a result of prayer, and would the pastor please bring some proof to show him. The pastor read the letter to us and we organized the 54 people who had been healed. We, along with our documentation, were taken by bus to a meeting with a group of about 20 doctors and professors.

There was total confusion upon our arrival. The Commissioner had assumed that there would be three or four of us—not 54! The place was small and they hadn't counted on that many. So the pastor went in with a few people. The larger group remained outside. The specialists carefully perused the files to see what types of tests, machines, etc. were used to determine our results.

Once they had finished, the Commissioner said to our pastor, "Apostle, we will work together with you." So we went home rejoicing.

People came nonstop to be healed and delivered. So, our pastor launched a large healing crusade every night for a month. Many were being. So many sick people were coming that our pastor (the Apostle) had several of them living in his home. I would go and cook for them, sometimes all day.

One day a well-known healing evangelist approached our pastor about helping him launch a similar healing crusade in the city of Jinja, which is at the source of the Nile River. On Monday our pastor announced that he was going to Jinja, but would return the next day. They loaded their truck with sound equipment. Sadly, we received a call midmorning that our pastor, the driver and his brother, and several other people had been killed in an auto accident. Their bodies were taken to the Lugazi Hospital.

We checked, and it was true. The whole city was shaken. Our church was full of broken-hearted people. The pastor's wife was phoned in Canada and told of his passing. She and some of their eight children caught planes to come to Uganda.

People were gathered in rooms all over the church property praying for God to resurrect our pastor. In Africa it is not uncommon for God to resurrect the dead. But that was not to be the case. He was later buried in his village.

CHAPTER 10 – A Ministry Is Born

In November of 1995 I was walking home from the main road to my house when I heard a voice that said, "Ruth, I'm calling you to minister to widows." I could hardly believe it. I looked to the left and to the right. It was dark, and no one was there. I was puzzled. I was so frightened that I ran all the way home.

I rushed to my room and thought to myself, *God wouldn't ask this of me. I am a widow myself! There are so many widows per capita in our country, how could I possibly meet their needs? I have needs of my own.*

Widows here are outcasts, jobless, and their children are not even in school. How can I tell them to come back to God?

But God said, "Ruth, their biggest need isn't money. Their hearts are far from me, even when they pray I don't hear them, because they pray in bitterness, unforgiveness, cursing, and hatred. Go show them my love. Tell them that there is hope; and that I'm here for them."

In January 1996 there was a conference hosted by Apostle Mulinde (Africa Camp). A group from Eldoret Township in Kenya attended the conference. I worked in the Accommodations Department and looked after them while they were with us. One of them, a young girl, said, "I would like for you to meet my mother. She also is a widow with a ministry to widows."

Later that year I received an invitation to go to Eldoret. Kenya and speak at a widows' conference. I asked God to give me the words to speak, and to help me. He was so faithful. He showed me how he had delivered me from unforgiveness, grief, mourning, loneliness, and more. He reminded me of how He'd brought me hope when I was hopeless. *"That's the hope I want you to give them,"* He said. *"Tell them I am faithful to forgive and to restore. Tell them to put their trust in me, and to stop praying worry-filled, prayers of unbelief and bitterness. That's why I cannot answer their prayers. Tell them to come to me, and that I will heal them, deliver them, and be a father to their children."*

During the conference another lady spoke about how unforgiveness binds you to the person you refuse to forgive. She explained that even when you are apart from that person, the spiritual bondage remains. Her message was a powerful word to me regarding my former mother-in-law.

When I returned home I went and bought some sugar and some salt as gifts to take to her. I had loved her like a mother. But when my husband died, she rejected me. I went to her home. She welcomed me, and we reconciled and once more became friends.

In 1999 I went to Pastor Frieda at *Victory Church* and told her my testimony, my experiences, what I'd learned, and what I felt God wanted me to do. I asked her what she felt I should do.

"Ruth," She said. "Your vision is from God. We have many widows in our churches but we leaders don't even understand them and what they face. Many of them feel unloved, and we don't know what to say to them. As God raises you up, they will listen to you. I would like to help you. We'll select a month that is open, and host an annual widows conference."

I called several widows. We formed a committee and

began to work on the details. We found a school in which we could conduct the first conference.

The first week of May 1999 we rented the Nakivubo Blue Primary school, arranged for housing, and promoted our event on the local radio station. Three hundred widows attended at our first meeting! I invited the lady who hosted me in Eldoret, Kenya to come and speak. We had deliverance, forgiveness, and five of the widows were born again including a Catholic, an Anglican, and a Muslim.

We challenged those widows to return to their churches and get engaged; to no longer be separate; to get involved in every activity and to help one another. Pastors from their churches told me later how pleased that they were to see the engagement of their widows in the activities of their churches.

They began to invite me to speak in their churches as well.

We held our conference the next year thereafter and began to spread out to the districts across the country.

In our conferences, we would ask attorneys and doctors to address the women too. They needed to be tested for AIDS; learn proper hygiene; be shown how to get medical help, and how to defend their legal rights.

We encouraged them to refrain from marriage until their hearts were healed.

In 2001, June Richards from *Kingsway Church* in Manchester, England came to Uganda. I was in a neighboring country, Rwanda when she came. She told a friend of mine that her ministry, *Deborah Arise International* in the U.K., mentored mothers to pray for their children, and to raise a godly generation. She said that she was looking for someone who could oversee that ministry to mothers in Uganda. My friend mentioned me to her and suggested that she contact me.

Rev. Richards contacted my pastor who explained that I was out of the country. She left a note asking me to contact her when I returned. She said she was leaving the county on Tuesday.

I came home on Monday. When I was given her message I went straight to the house where she was staying where I met her, and we shared our visions with each other. She told me the vision of her ministry which was to get women, particularly mothers, to pray for the next generation.

She asked what I did. I explained that my ministry was called *Widows Intercessors International.*

She pulled out a paper on which she'd written a prophecy she had received in Brazil. It said widows would play a great part in praying for the young people. "This is a divine appointment. Would you coordinate our ministry in Uganda?" She asked.

I told her, "Yes, I will."

That same year we had our conference in Mukono District. I took an attorney with me to teach the widows their legal rights. We had workshops for married people, widows, men, women, youth and children. NOTE: In our conferences we provide ministry to the whole body of Christ.

In that conference I encouraged our widows to pray and to organize themselves to bless their districts. I encouraged them to consider ways that they might do so. One of the elderly widows, who was toothless said,

"Pastor, if I can get a cow, I will care for it. And when that cow gives birth to a calf, I will sell the milk and have some left for my grandchildren. It will help support me and my family."

At my workshop I told her story. I challenged them to do more than merely pray. We need to also apply ourselves in meaningful ways to support our families. I explained that while it is true that God loves to bless us, it's also true that we need to recognized and accept our own responsibilities to bless others. Faith without works is dead.

The attorney I had taken with me handed me a note that read, "I will give her the cow." I read the note aloud to the entire group and they were ecstatic. Filled with joy, they jumped to their feet, cheered and clapped their hands.

When the conference ended, I was given the money for the cow. I drove it back to that village and placed it in the hands of the widow's pastor saying, "Pastor, please take this money and buy the cow." He did.

To own that cow was life-changing for that dear elderly widow and her family. Later I was given a picture of her and her cow.

In 2002, I invited June Richards to return to Uganda and speak for us at our national conference. At that conference, June and another lady who had accompanied her from the U.K. laid hands on me and commissioned me as Uganda's national coordinator for *Deborah Arise International.*

Our conference ended on Saturday. The next day I invited those ladies to attend my church. When we walked in, the lady who had accompanied June Richards to Uganda began to weep. For what, we did not know. When she was able to speak, we asked her why she was crying. She said, "The Holy Spirit spoke to me that you are not to coordinate *Deborah Arise* just in your nation of Uganda, but in the whole African continent."

When they met my senior pastor, they told her what they sensed the Holy Spirit had told them. My pastor said, "Go ahead. Let's commission her to do so now." They did.

CHAPTER 11 – Off To England

Throughout 2002 we traveled across our nation ministering to people, conducting days of prayer in each district, and establishing the *Deborah Arise* vision.

In 2003, June graciously invited me to speak in Manchester, England. She organized women's meetings for me to share what God was doing with our *Widows Intercession* and *Deborah Arise International* ministries in Africa.

During my time in England, we flew from Manchester to another city, where I was to teach. I prayed, "God, this is my first trip to England. I don't have anything to take with me to offer the people." I knew that other ministers made audio CDs, video DVDs, books and other resources available, but I had nothing but 23 simple brochures that described our work. I had nothing with which to garner support for my ministry.

While I was praying with two prayer partners in my room, I felt the Lord say, "Ruth, take them my Word. They need my Word. The rest will follow." In obedience to the Lord, I placed the brochures, as I was directed, on the table in the back of the auditorium. After the meeting I noticed that they were all gone.

When we returned to Manchester, I received an email from a lady named Christine Reading. She wrote, "I picked up your brochure at the church. I am so excited about what you are doing in Uganda. I've been traveling for over 15 years to do ministry in Troro, Uganda. When I returned home with your brochure I had a dream.

In the dream I was in my kitchen preparing food for

guests, but the food wasn't enough. Then you appeared (in my dream) standing beside me in my kitchen. You joined in my work and as we worked together, there was enough food for my guests. I feel we must talk. Please tell me where you are staying in Manchester, I will drive over to see you." She did.

As Christine and I sat and talked that day I showed her the photo of the happy elderly toothless widow and her cow. She said, "Ruth, do you mean that one cow can bring that much joy and provision for a family?" I assured her that it could and it does. I said, "That widow looks younger, is in better health, and is able to care for her family because of that single cow."

When Christine returned home, she emailed me again saying, "Ruth, I have the money to buy five cows for widows. But how do you travel to those places?"

I explained that I used public transportation, bicycles, motor bikes, private transportation, and quite often walked long distances—especially in places where there were no roads."

She answered, "God will bless you. Soon you will own a car so you can get to them quickly."

I returned home rejoicing, with the money to buy five cows. Upon my arrival we bought five cows and distributed them to five districts. We were ecstatic to have cows in six districts!

Here is the process. When a cow gives birth, the owner of the cow keeps the calf and gives the cow to another needy widow. It's like a chain of blessing. They know that the cow they own is not theirs alone, but for the entire group.

One day Christine called from the U.K. and asked, "Ruth, why not consider piglets?" I thought: *that would be great. One sow can give birth to as many as 8 or 10 piglets!* So we began raising money to buy piglets for widows in the villages. Before long, we had bought and distributed 120 piglets to the widows in the villages! They were greatly encouraged.

When the piglets grew and gave birth, they could sell the young ones and earn income.

In 2006 Christine Reading encouraged us to buy land and build a center. I told her that was something in my long-range vision. It would be a place where people could come and cultivate the land (for food), pray, share, and be discipled. It would also be a place where we could build a home for homeless elderly widows, many of whom are incapable of cultivating land, and growing their own food to live out their lives with dignity.

God soon provided the money and we bought ten acres of land. The widows were excited when we explained to them that this land was theirs. About that time the Lord also provided us with a minibus (a van) to enable us to go to the villages to distribute food and clothing more quickly and easily.

We built a two room building on the new land, one room for the ministry office and the other for the supplies and equipment necessary to tend the land.

From there we built two rooms for our workers, and started a pig project.

One widow, a friend of mine, gave us one cow; and we bought a second one. The cows and the pigs began to give birth and God began to spread the blessings around.

As I write this book today we have cows in 12 districts.

Christine sent over sewing machines which we set up in Mityana District. There they have a cow, piglets, a sewing center and workshop where widows are taught to sew. We also bought three goats for our widows in Bussi, which is an island in the Wakiso District.

We continue to pray over the widows, provide counseling for them, and encourage them. We have an office for our ministry headquarters on Williams Street in Kampala City. The building is called *Get In House*. That's where widows gather for prayer, to be prayed for, to be encouraged, informed, and inspired.

CHAPTER 12 – Today And Tomorrow

Recently I had the idea to teach the widows how to make craft items to sell for their support. A talented lady agreed to show them how to make the crafts. A family in the U.K. who heard what we were doing and what we needed donated the money to buy a machine that would cut thick paper, from which the crafts are made. The craft effort is quite successful now.

In 2012, when I visited the U.K. a wonderful generous couple, Peter and Ann, adopted the village of Lira, which is one of our northern villages on the river. Many men have died and have left a great many widows and orphans. I told Peter and Ann that we have a well-established ministry in Lira.

Last year when Peter and Ann visited us we took them along with the lady who taught us to make crafts to Lira. They had brought materials with which craft items could be made. We had a wonderful conference. The women wanted to learn, so they came out in big numbers.

Upon seeing the need, Peter and Anne encouraged the widows to do organic farming. All of the widows could benefit from growing their own food. They visited Kenya where they were taught the best procedures to get the greatest harvest from the land. They even arranged for the widows to have the equipment to make hand-made bricks for construction projects. Widows had always been society's outcasts, homeless, and helpless. They had nothing with which they could care for themselves and their children.

This is even more important when one realizes that in the past, when a widow's children came to her to ask for money, her response was typically, "You know that we have no money since your father died."

Because of this, many of them saw their children turn against them and in some cases abandon them. As you drive the city streets today you see homeless children and teens fighting for survival. When you ask about their families, they explain that they have a mother, but they don't have a father. When their mother could no longer feed and support them, they ran away to live on the streets.

As we look to the future to see what God has planned for us we will certainly face challenges, like I did when I lost my darling youngest daughter, at the young age of 30, in 2009. It was quite a challenge that caused me to even want to leave the ministry. But God encouraged and strengthened me, and I continue to this day.

Dear reader, thank you so much for reading my story. I pray that something I've shared with you will stir you to greater love and service of our King Jesus. I also pray that the victories I've experienced over the challenges that I have faced, will encourage you to know that God will strengthen and guide you through the challenges that lie before you. He is a faithful Father.

As I've shared, because of war, AIDS, and other diseases, my beloved Uganda has a disproportionate number of widows and orphans who suffer day by day. They need our help. We must reach them not only with the wonderful gospel of Christ, but equip them to find health, the skills, and the encouragement that they need to go on. They need no longer live as outcasts.

At this time, we have almost 3,000 widows that we minister to throughout the 28 districts. Many of them face terrible conditions, without medical care or families to care for them. We are praying and working to build a large center in which we can house and provide for them. At the moment we are caring for 24 elderly widows in seven districts. Some widows are abused and have no one to fight for them in court.

Perhaps now that you know our struggle, you may as many do, feel led to pray for and to invest in our ministry. One of the challenges ministries in developing nations like ours have is to make it possible for Western Christians to safely contribute to our support, and know that every cent they invest safely reaches us.

Our American office:

To make this possible in the United States, Alice and Eddie Smith and the *U. S. Prayer Center* in Houston, Texas provide a contact point and procedures to get your kingdom investment to us. To take advantage of that please mail your income tax-deductible checks or money orders payable to:

U.S. Prayer Center
7710-T Cherry Park Dr, Ste 224
Houston, TX 77095

PLEASE NOTE: To avoid any tax issues do not write on your check's "For" line. Instead, DO include a note along with your check saying: "For Pastor Ruth Mwagalwa in Uganda," and the *U.S. Prayer Center* will forward your gift to us.

Our U.K. Office:

If our U.K. address is more appropriate for your use, make your checks and/or International money orders payable to:
Christine Reading
Email:chrisreading001@ntlworld.com
Phone 01252 512113
Bank account details: *Open Door Missions International*
Account number 20446459
Sort Code 20-61-82,
Barclays Bank,
North Farnborough Branch.

Our Ugandan Offices

Ruth Mwagalwa
Account number: 0150102113201
Standard Chartered Bank
5 Speke Road, PO BOX 7111 Kampala
Uganda

Swift code SCBLUGKA

Tel: +256-772429656
+256-312371391,
Email: ruthmwagalwa@yahoo.com
Website: www.WidowsMinistryUG.org
Bank account details:
Widows Intercessors Ministries
Account: 01101020591870
DFCU Bank
Nsabya branch, Kampala

Uganda

We pray God's richest blessings on you and yours!

Ruth Mwagalwa